The Shores of Time

Elle Daviou

CLOVER+CRYSTALLINUM
PUBLISHING

ISBN: 978-1-943337-82-8
pISBN: 978-1-943337-80-4
eISBN: 978-1-943337-81-1
Any references to historical events, real people, or real places are used fictitiously. Names, characters, and places are products of the author's imagination.

Published by: Clover + Crystallinum Publishing
Book Design - Cover & Interior

www.elledaviau.com/clover-crystallinum-publishing

Author website: http://www.elledaviau.com

Printed in the United States of America
Seattle, Washington

You're attracted to the poison...
that kills you.

Elle Daviau

The Shores of Time

The loves we experience
time and time again
how they crash and retreat
with the tide of emotions that run
through us—
bobbing and weaving under the depths,
sometimes leaving marks
and slashes
as the bad ones inevitably roll in.

They'll kiss us with sweet lips,
laced with poison
meant to deceive us
and dilute our minds in false promise.
They lure us in
to capture our hearts
on the tides
of the shores of time.

And this is what they did to me.

The shores of time live deep in all of us.
If you look closely,
it's always there.

~ *Elle Daviau*

The Shores of Time

Elle Daviau

CLOVER+CRYSTALLINUM
PUBLISHING

The Shores of Time

Elle Daviau

fairy floss

Left with your strain of
benevolence,
iridescent
fairy floss caught up
in your throat, taking away
every last breath of your
heart, gasping.

I walked over to the place where life
grows
and couldn't help
but let my cotton candy heart
wither through my skin
giving away my life,
to allow another to discover theirs.

Elle Daviau

What's Love Like?

I try to feel it.
The shivers.
The butterflies below my ribs,
disrupting the concentrated
flow of life,

dopamine releases.

The taste of sweet sugar—
a cocoon around me,
but when I look at your earthy eyes,

it only tastes like salt to me.

Elle Daviau

I Kissed Him at The Base of The Cherry Tree

I'm tired of liking
someone and them not
liking me back.
   It's like the trees loving
         the breeze,
   but the wind
         never waits

         for someone like me.

Elle Daviau

Elle Daviau

English Poison Ivy

Her eyes were
green.
The way ivy crawled
up trees.
And she took me around my neck.

I could never
let her go after that.

Elle Daviau

He Says I Taste Like Strawberry Pudding

I guess it's quite obvious, with the way the
mountain stares,
The way the ocean kisses my toes
before he's ripped away
from my side.
The way the breeze travels
through my hair just to remind me
he'll always be with me.

I guess when I saw the fire
in your eyes I assumed you'd singe my heart.
But that stone-cold look of yours
when you told me
you loved me
showed me I had everything
wrong from the start.

Elle Daviau

Ruby Girls

Only sad cancers
cry a lot.
But I can't help but be a
                    sad girl
when everyone disappoints my high
expectations
                    all the time.

Elle Daviau

Elle Daviau

After You Left Me

Now I've found a boy
who treats me nice

and you have a girl
with a rotten mind

but I'm all you dream
about when you fall asleep.

So, she dyed her hair blonde
for when she turns
over and you hold her,
she could look
just like me.

Elle Daviau

Honeybee

It was real cruel of him
     to mess with her emotions,
     him knowing
     that inside,
     she was made of butterflies
     and day-dreams
     and magic.

And this all affected her
     right to that inside core.
     The butterflies die young
     the dreams become terrors
     and she lost all mysticism,
     as she was doomed
     to become completely ordinary.

Elle Daviau

Elle Daviau

He Only Says He Loves Me When He Touches Me

he wants her body,
not her mind.

Elle Daviau

Elle Daveau

sweet like cherry pie

He let me go,
easily,
  softly.

The way a flower dies.

Elle Daviau

Elle Daviau

When I Was Lost in the Corn Maze

She forgot to stop
focusing on things that don't
matter, things like you

forgetting her way
and losing solace
she became a lost
soul when the moon
hit its peak,
searching through the
rows upon rows of leaves on tall stocks
induced exhaustion
as the moon whispered
down to her,

>   *he will not be*
>   *coming back.*

Elle Daviau

Sugar Plum Memories

They have gone
and once you heal,
the memory of yourself can only exist
with them.
You have changed,
shedding your chrysalis
for another time,
now your view of the world changes.
Up in the sky,
above the others left stagnant
in the sugar plum trees
you leave yourself behind
you are no longer that person,
nor do you want to be.

Elle Daviau

Blue Tint All Over Again

She became the kind
of girl
that only loves those
who don't
love her back.

Elle Daviau

He Calls Me Sunrise

I went to the park on Thursday.

And I met someone new
he had deep eyes full with
cobalt blue.

We went down to the old shed house,
by the water, and next to the
meadows.

We moved and just existed.
I pretended he was my twin flame.

While I drank the last of his
juice box, he laid me down
to sleep.

Civil dusk came quickly, and
sunrise came too soon.

When he lifted up my sheet,
atop my bed of flowers,
he realized he'd never
live up to me,

and the dreamy colors
that glazed my skies.

But that didn't matter because
with him

I was free.

Elle Daviau

Luna Moths in the Summertime

I'd like to think,
that maybe one day we can sit
side by side
and imagine the
shipwrecked memories that fill
one another's eyes.
We'll sit
until the water washes over
all the setback guilt,
and bring in the resurrection
of our consciousness
as the golden heat washes over my
insecurities and cultivated cries.

Elle Daviau

Elle Daviau

Fuchsia Love

He couldn't help but to involve
     other people and confess
     untrue emotions
     when his soul connected
     to hers.

     Trepidation lost him
     his greatest love,

       his only love.

Elle Daviau

Candy Lane

Barefoot she walks,
through the canopy of the trees,

every branch brushing her arm,

the world crushing beneath her feet.
Climbing up through the pathway that
she carved up her leg,
there's resonance of
memories scattered, a baseball here,
a tea cup there, these moments have left their
mark
and now have a place to stay;
but the most profound thing
was the rope that hung
from the oak tree.
It wasn't sinister,
it represented completion,
when she found that the rope had been
taken away,

gratitude was lost,

and all memories were reserved for the
time being.

Elle Daviau

His Girl

Do you think
we're meant to be
alone?

Leave our hearts lost
in the wind when we only hold
light for another?

Elle Daviau

Soft Honeydew

I've grown quiet
as you've taken away
all the silence.

All my peace.

Elle Daviau

Elle Davieu

a touch point extraction for all my inspiration ♡

Part 1

You laid among the garden flowers
and gave yourself away.

Elle Daviau

Logan

Part 2

I remember the blue in your eyes,
the slightest hint of grey

You've always been there for me
at my side.

The sunlight soaks into you,

I knew we didn't have forever
together.

Softly sweeping through the grass,

you told me this was it.

And I felt it, as

you laid among the clovers in the grass
and gave yourself away.

Elle Daviau

Elle Davian

Silk Milk

I miss the worlds I've
known,

how the sun
misses the moon
in the daylight sky.

Elle Daviau

Elle Daviau

Light in My Life

Some things look
best at night

The stars
bursting against
the black sky.

The moon
aglow in all
of its glory.

And you,
whispering me
back to life
like a firefly
who's lost its glow.

Elle Daviau

Elle Davian

Violet Pearl

Next time I'll
go to the stars.

You were always such a soulful creature.
I think that's where I might find you.

Elle Daviau

Elle Davieau

Dreaming

If only you could dream.
You would find
that dreaming with me
would take you to the blackest
parts of the universe,
where the edge
of your existence
struggles
to grasp my heart.

Elle Daviau

Ellis

She's not
afraid of the boys
like the other
girls are.

Elle Daviau

Elle Davian

First Quarter, Waxing Moon

She had this tendency
to pick up the broken.
And she, the moon,
cast her delusions
into their eyes
to block out the bad,
to make things seem
well again.

Elle Daviau

Oceanus

Your kind heart pulls me in
when the sun goes down

and the crystals light up
in the green horizon.

Elle Daviau

When a Lion Loves a Lamb

Her boyfriend is a biker,
his friends told her
she was this innocent flower,
but they acted afraid
of her.

It was as if
they thought she was going to tear
their hearts out.
Or maybe that he would to her.

Elle Daviau

Elle Davian

It Only Tastes Like Salt to Me

Nobody wanted to hold
her hand like how she wanted
to deeply hold theirs.

Elle Daviau

He Was an Aquarius, The Wrong Kind

Part 1

Soon enough
you're going to get tired of
my walls
and right then,
that's when I'll let you in.
But
you'll be gone
and yet again
I've let my trust issues
get in the way
of my broken
heart's repair.

Elle Daviau

and i am a cancer…
Part 2

I never understand why I have a broken
heart each time.

But then,
I ask my walls
and they remind me
that it's
     safer alone.

Elle Daviau

Wishes That Just Don't Come True

Living in my chapter five page thirteen.

There, I have a lot of ideas
on what life is like.

        In my chapter five
      page thirteen:

We live a beautiful life down by the
lagoon.

      In chapter five page thirteen:

We share unconditional love.
Everlasting.

      Chapter five page thirteen:

You're the one I'll always want.

ch 5 pg 13:

The problem is,
you won't always want me.

Elle Daviau

Elle Daviau

Honey Pie Kind of Love.
Just Like You.

He had only half
a heart,
the rest was made out of
where the crystals
coalesced
on the stars, that fell
from the sky on each night
he felt lonely.

Crying
himself into his slumber
and the starlight
filled each break I chipped
into him,
trying to fix
what had already been broken.

Elle Daviau

Elle Davieu

A Shade Lighter Than Scarlet

But the colors changed
their hue &
I could never
remember what it was
    like to love you
        after that.

Elle Daviau

Elle Davian

Him and His Friends Had Motorcycles and He Had Tattoos

He holds me
and tells me he loves me
he says I'm his truest love.
And if there was a world without me,
he couldn't survive another day.

Elle Daviau

Elle Davian

"Oi, Blondie," he said.

"You remind me of my ex
a little different,
but
almost exact."

Elle Daviau

i was putting on my almond milk lotion

And he called her crying last night,
talking about how she doesn't care
about him.
But he hadn't even acknowledged her
for weeks.
She was the one making sure
he was okay,
but he was just gone.

    She listened
to every word
and when he was done,
it took all her strength to draw back
every rational thought she had.
And,
"I love you, you know," was the only
thing she could possibly say after that.

Elle Daviau

i just want my strawberry milkshake

I'm enchanting &
pretty when I cry & now I
do it all the time.

Elle Daviau

It's Hard to Communicate

It's fire in my mouth
and cotton in my lungs.
The words I say to you, when
I try to make you feel something,

so you know
what you're doing
is hurting me.

Elle Daviau

The Fool

Only a few words from you
can make me fall apart.

And it feels like walking
towards the sunrise, dazed by the light.

Feels like skin submerged in cool water—
the water that now drips down my hair.

I reach out to touch
the shadow across your face.

My eyes locked on yours, I take one step
closer, falling off the cliff.

I become the light,
and you never existed.

Elle Daviau

The Truest Friend

I thought he was so peculiar
                                    at first.

But now,
            I don't understand
        how one person
    got to become so important
                                to me.

Elle Daviau

Elle Davieu

Cold-Blooded Scorpio

I laid at rest among the gravel,
the seabirds
swooping and cooing at me,
trying to get me up from my state of
distress.
It was the mental suffering that cut right
through my skin
and crept under my spine
between each vertebrae I felt it,
paralyzing me from the thought of
losing you.
I surrendered to the sea
and you became the air.

Elle Daviau

A Baby Pepsi-Cola

I'm done crying
and hurting.

   And I'm tired
of being sad

       about you.

Elle Daviau

K.

I have a lot of things to say to you,
like how I love art,
& flowers
& how I love spending time with you,
all the time.
but you don't care
for the things I talk about.
My words invoke the anger in you.

I'm stuck
between I don't know
what to say

& I don't want
to stop talking to you.

Elle Daviau

Like Life in the Ocean

Loving him is like drowning.

Blind from the beautiful view as a
monster lures her down into the dark
depths.

I'm lost in a shadowy sea

tossing about in heaps of kelp, a
frozen body waits.

Bars guard the cave opening, doused in
barnacles, they cut deep through soft skin.

I'm awake now,

gasping for air leaves her lungs hopeless
and renders them useless—like they've
forgotten how to breathe.

Muscles release, fingers lose their tension,
hands tighten around her wrists, pulling
her in.

I let go.

Her last glimpse of daylight passes by and all too soon he has her in his grip.

She's given herself over to a devil, dressed in the shell of a man she loves.

Elle Daviau

Elle Daviau

I Have Beautiful Eyes and Blonde Hair

I looked at him with endearment,
in love with my best friend.
He knows.

He tells me all about her,
all the time: his ex.

I wish I didn't love him,
but I just don't love him enough
                    to let him go.

Elle Daviau

Love

I don't understand it
so I never expect
to have it.

Elle Daviau

Elle Davieu

Lavender Moonlight

How could I not be
spiritual when the stars
are placed in my eyes.

Elle Daviau

Elle Davieau

Lilac Cotton

She was waiting
    for the maple leaves to fall,
    with anticipation
    in her cotton candy
    heart.

Now,
    the silent voice,
    whispering in her ear that
    today is the yesterday from
    past lives when the Piper
    called and the children
    were taken away.

Soon,
    prolonged sorrows
    of how she keeps missing
    every window
    of when it is time to reap
    what she had sown.

The resurrection of those
    who have inward eyes,
    blind to the surrounding world,
    yet catching the faint glimpse

of the red cornelia
    saying its last goodbye
    until the morning rise.

And let those who have mystic minds
    find the ones pleading
    with their voodoo calls
    to be cured
    by burning a hole
    through the lilac
    crystallized sugar blue
    resting just below
    her fiberglass bones.

Until the light burns out
    and it becomes dark
    and new
    once again.

Elle Daviau

Mirrored Bones

I briefly remember waking up;
    rubbing alcohol christening the air
& my vision consumed by black.

It wasn't the sudden head rush
    that startled me,
    only the light of which she was,
    guiding me back into my own
    subconscious thoughts.

Her touch is ice on your skin,
    the same kind that fills her heart.
    She's the smell of green tea,
    raspberry diet pills
    & coffee beans.

The sound of graphite lead on walls,
    caps twisting
    & weighted numbers beeping.
    A flavor so bright and colorful
    that you end up tasting everything
    you love, but taking away
    all that you are.

Leaving you only with a frame
    of bones & your golden accord.

Elle Daviau

Darling

She will soon learn
those people on her phone
are not all that important.

Elle Daviau

Sunflowers Rise with the Morning Sun

She remembers this moment,
when something really good happened.

She also remembers she learned
how easily it was
taken away.

Elle Daviau

Wild Flowers

At the base of my thoughts you'll find
the discarded petals now all dried from
the times when I questioned if you had the
strength to mend the tears in your thread
thin insecurity;
    leading to me to think that I had
        done you wrong.

Cotton wells up in the crown of my pith,
making its way through the
canopy fears that cloud over me when your
    soft touch brushes my blades
        of eternal life.

We will only know, after the fringed
bleeding heart blooms, the answers to
our uncertainty. Of whether we both can
contribute to start building the roots of
which we live on or if the flames you carry
on your charcoaled ash lie on the grave of
    where I once stood, grimly
        in my hesitant ground.

Elle Daviau

Pink Cocoa Cupcake

And how do they make
you feel? Those people you say
you don't care about.

Elle Daviau

Temperance at the Altar

With light step, I search
through my memories careful not to
pass over where
Eros
makes the cursed floor boards
scream.

Guiding me with artificial light,
I looked to the moon to show me the
map coded in theban symbols
just under his glitter armor
but glamoured by his
delusions,

I trip on the marble staircase and
look up with total defeat in my eyes,
while the cloaked figure looks
sideways, lurking.
Watching me over the edge of the
chalice
held by the slow moving,
mysterious horseman,
and the witching hour moves on.

I misplace my balance over the now
scarlet glazed ice from the fallen
China cabinet.

It feeds up into the flesh
  of my soul.
As I look down,
      a gaze of
  unrest settles on my face
          and the reconstruction
  of the reaping skeleton
    dilutes my mind.

Forgetting where we have once come
    and now faced with my decision
of whether I will go.

Neither it be a path I follow
    nor a gate I must enter,
I trust my transition into the next
          renewal rest
  and await the sun of immortality.
      She'll rise from her grave
and flood the
          prism windows
  with her
          rosy waves.

Let her heat crash onto my
    bathroom floor
as I wake from my
      eternal sleep.

Elle Daviau

Tanzanite Crystal Skies

I would tell her that although it is
        important to put her trust
into those she meets,
        it is just as important to not
            hand out her dahlia credence
                to all the hexing eyes
she trips over, time-after-time.

I would warn her not to look too far into the
wishing well
            because it's hard to yell
        from twenty feet down.

    Reciting wish-after-wish
to the dark,
wishing,
that he will come back
to pull you out,
but only realizing you're
        down…
                down…
            down so far, is because of he
who is standing
        at your side.

I would remind her that being filled
with her cynical fairy tales;
    the ones where the strawberry moon is
resting in her Tanzanite crystal skies–
    the ones where the fool takes another

Step off into the sunsetted cliff;
    and where cyclic death is never written
at the end of the
    hero's journey–
    it is not to be brought into disrepute,
    but to be recognized as the hero for
    catching her before she falls into their
      screaming waters
        full of sugar-coated lies.

Elle Daviau

Peaches & Cream

Lonely Atlanta,
Georgia. Blinding me from the
new moon, my starlight.

Elle Daviau

Little Red

The caterpillar let in the rouge
kind of sadness
while he closed his eyes
and wrapped himself up.

But stretched his wings
as he woke
with the light
of a thousand stars.

Elle Daviau

I Saw the Moon Last Night

And yet, we are mistaken,

> we think we love
> the Milky Way galaxy
>> that is meant to keep the stars
>> and planets apart…

>>> meant to keep us apart.

Elle Daviau

Elle Davian

The Beauty in Me Sleeps

It came to me in a dream
He always comes back to me when
    he gets bored with her.

And that's the reason
I let him go.

Elle Daviau

Elle Daviau

His Shadow

The crystals and rocks cried
    the water down their face
when the rain came through.
    Breaking their own hearts at the
waves, crushing them together.
    Encapsulating the feeling that
brought each one of them there.
    The cat swayed
through the window
    before the humans
        came back.
    His paws made so little of a
sound that they whispered
into the small opening.
    He jumped down but when the
leaves on the ground connected
    with his outreached paws,
they called out to the humans,
    and the cat knew his adventure
had finally come to an end.

Elle Daviau

133

Elle Daviau

Transcendence

Haven't you heard of the beautiful
things? Where the flowers bloom in the
places untouched;
    where you have not yet touched my
                  heart.
    Where motions are felt, and lives will
die, and yet, they bloom again.
    Where death is just a passage onto the
new season.
    There's a message in that,
    and it says:
    time will go on and you will love
                again.

Elle Daviau

Elle Davian

Shells in Sand, & I'm Alone Again

      I turned onto
   the stretch of rocks where the houses
disappeared,
      knocking the shells and stones
   back into their place,
trickling back to their home.

      I placed my steps carefully,
   angling the souls of my bare feet
off the sharpest rocks.

      A glowing orange
   wedged in the sand lifted my eyes.
The squirrel
      locked his eyes with mine,
   and trudged away
with his gatherings.

    Elle Daviau

You're Sweet Like Sugar to Me

The stiffness of your hand was
                    condensing my air:

    I could only hope
that you wouldn't crush me
under all your
    desolation.

Elle Daviau

Elle Daviau

Pretty June Bugs

Butterflies, they all
caramelize when I'm away
from innocent, you.

Elle Daviau

The Rose Moon

Part 3

They say she was born in the
    strawberry fields.

You could get lost in her turquoise eyes
    Almost missing the glamourous sight
    of her golden hair—

a sad girl with the most beautiful soul.

The kind of soul with an aura that
       shined iridescent blue.

She didn't talk a lot but had many
      things to say.

She met a boy, in her youth.
    A boy with raven hair and fair skin.

He, a dangerous soul.
    She, pure of heart.

Time goes by before she gets a letter
      "I don't want to see you again."
                 - Him

He left without a trace of explanation.

His reason, he only knew:
                she was too much,
    too beautiful to touch,
                    to look at,
              to be next to,
                        to be *with*.

He could never live up to that kind of
beauty.

Unknowingly leaving her forever
    broken.

    After that day,
                she was gone.

        Some say
        she ventured out to find him.

Most others say, she went back to the
strawberry fields,

and there, she laid atop the earth
    and gave herself away.

Elle Daviau

143

Yayo and His Raspberry Highs

I never liked it
    your infatuation with it…
    the white dust concealed behind
    your eyes,
    on the bliss point of your skin.
    It was there forever
    like the clouds in the sky.

I think it really got to me when I
realized you'd never love me
like that:
    in any way possible,
    so strong of a connection,
    no matter what it did to you.

And that was exactly the way that
I loved you.

Elle Daviau

I Feel Reborn Today
part 1

In the moon's eyes
I'll stay by your side and
the lost city of Atlantis will sink
once again.

I won't forget you
in the depths of my heart,
nor at the edge
of the sea, drifting
along the shore of my mind.

And the last afterlife
that you told me about,
Summerland,
will capture the souls of past lives
and feed them with the ignited pain,
right out of your hand.

I conceptualized
the thought
of going down into Asphodel Meadows,
but I would never see you again,
stretching the lies
that you once thought
would widow me.

May the eyes of Neptune
shine light
on that which you have done,
merciful
of the elegance you brought,
cutting through the grieving decay
that has fallen upon
my heart.

Elle Daviau

Tropico Verde

part 2

I'll cross the tides and walk into your
Asphodel Meadows,
forever scared with the etching
that your waves cause
when they crash into my ribs,
where I used to detain Atlantis,
lost in my heart...

Elle Daviau

One Ol' Kiss and It'll All Be Better

She is regretful
and disillusioned.

But she's not guilty
for the things she didn't do.

When confronted with the way you felt
she knew you were apologetic
as you should be.

Elle Daviau

The Rain Witch

The things you did
continue to get covered up
by the amethyst haze that
        wants to forget
                what you did.

Elle Daviau

He Uses Me for What He Wants

It's time slowing to a catastrophic halt. Or is
it a beautiful one?
There is nothing outside of the feeling, all
senses are numb.
       Touch: the only exception.

Warmth seeped into me just as fast as
          my cold heart fills you.
I don't think you quite get it yet.
You're in love with me,
but I'm unsure of you.

It's not a game
even though it feels like one.
And it's much more than a crush,
even when you leave me
to fill in the blanks.

Mirror images of each other,
       yin and yang.
       Some sort of cosmic rush.
It's funny how things led up to where we
are now,
but I'm not sure where we're going.

Things blow up.
       They settle down.

Somewhere along the way,
it all worked out.
I know...

      No,
         I think
I'm in love with you
      I'm just not sure how.

Elle Daviau

Elle Daviau

Sugar Burnt My Tongue When I Got a Taste of You

You're drowning,
you know how to swim
but she's the one pulling you down.
I can't save you,
it's up to you.
You could drown with her
or you could follow my light.
I'll lead the way,
but you have to make
your own decision,
and so do I.

Elle Daviau

The Crystal Sky

It's a glamourous
    world upon the ocean floor,
    the dimming sunlight
    shimmering against water
    that forms a crystal sky.
But prolonged dreams
      of these
    are his artifice.
With le bête noire waiting
    for you when you return, changed.
Falling awake
    into the arms
    of the beast himself.
Night terrors
    and reality
    can no longer separate
      in the Sea of Serenity,
      where you so wished to be.

Elle Daviau

Elle Daviau

The Sunlight Witch

Maybe I've just seen your face too many
times in my dreams;
where maybe, the skylight clouds continue
to roll in
and spread their amethyst haze over top
of the things you did;
where the cotton in my mouth builds up
when I say your name,
leaving me with my amnesia and your
crystal glow that seems to bleed
into the dazed salt of my eyes.

Elle Daviau

Sugarcane Syrup

I don't want to lose
you but you're gone now and that
makes me obsolete.

Elle Daviau

The Water Witch

I don't want you to see,
not only how wicked I am, but the
innocence.
Hidden in my good lies the bad.
Everywhere my light shines
is a shadow, with every shade
of color behind.
If I let you get too close
you'll see it,
because you'll only realize
the harrowing curse
I put over you when it's
too late to go back.

Elle Daviau

On a Spiritual Level

I don't think
he'll ever understand
how he makes me
feel.

Elle Daviau

Unrequited

You see me.
Watch me.

You're stardust on my
radar,
but I'm a star.
You stalk me.

I don't notice
as things becomes strange.
Hauntingly you move.

Your voice whispers
from corners.

Regrettably, I ignore you.
Because it's all I know.

Anger evolves you
and I don't recognize you anymore,
the lonely guy in the back of the room.

Offhanded comments become threats.

I told you I don't feel that way about you.

      You do for me.
I see it coming.
No, maybe I don't,
but through your words
and your presence, I know
I should have.
      Scared for my life.

You tear me down.
and bring me back.
And the moment
I let my guard down; you decide
you'd shoot me up.

Elle Daviau

Elle Davian

The Fear of Love

Good people can do bad things.
Bad people can trick you
into thinking that they've
changed.
But the most important people in this world
are the ones who can see
                    straight through
                              that front line.
Those who know what your intentions are.

                    The funny thing is...
            everyone wants to be friends
                    with those people,
                    but nobody is.

Elle Daviau

Elle Daviau

The Milk Moon

No, I haven't cried
over him for a while.

But I'm just a little too dark,

and mellow,

and mysterious
for someone like you.

Elle Daviau

Elle Daviau

I Just Want You to Stay Longer

People told her she needed to love herself,
then people would love her,
but she already did,
it just made her sad
that nobody else did.

Elle Daviau

Peaceful Warrior

I chase your light,
but the light travels
a star, and this star
is already dead.

Elle Daviau

J.

She already knew what the next one's name would start with,

it was her lucky letter.

Elle Daviau

Star Bright

Oh, but if I had the stars, I would play
into the night, I would toy with the moons
of Jupiter and
I would…

I would bring
starlight in through my eyes.

Elle Daviau

Honey Bunches

What are you doing to me?
You've got me in a box.
It's locked.
I have a key and you do, too.
But I have not yet ascertained
if you won't let me out
or if I'm the one that wants to stay.

Elle Daviau

The Curse of Cupido

And yes,
I shall continue to trip
down the path that the arrow of Eros
has set out for me; inevitably
crossing through
                    the darkest waters
                    and the most sorrow skies.

Elle Daviau

I'm a Bottle Blonde Girl

I can't believe
how they move on to the next Barbie
                like they're all the same
                like they're all like me
                or just like her.

Elle Daviau

Regret

I think sometimes, of the memories through which started our downfall.

The wishful vibrance that colored them, only to be turned to the grey that began to swell up in the middle of your green eyes.

When my vines started to fill your chest and out the top of your lungs, it brought back the vacant flesh and the scarlet heart, breathing right below your ribcage.

You reaped every flower I have sown, but slowly paralyzed me from the next eternal season, as my Luna Moths flew south you forced me to stay.

Then you brought in the confused skies and your waters full of agony and torture, but it wasn't I who hurt you, it was what you did to yourself that cut the most.

After my flowers had all wilted, so did you.

The lost feeling that your Boston Red Sox cap brought when you had gone was everything I avoided from the start.

And when my continuous wish for you to come back didn't work, I began to forget what it was like to touch the matte velvet of your face.

The morning bird is what you hoped to be, so you could get away from this life.

As it became your reality in an instant, a storm of dread slowly followed onto those you left; a constant crushing causing all to crumble. My vines that gave you life were to be cut free from where your body rests, leaving them forever scarred, and forever broken.

Only remembering what it was like to look into your trench fields, surrounded by your clarity waters.

I didn't want to let go.

But the minute you pulled the trigger to rip your heart out, is when your regret set in and I knew we could never go back.

Elle Daviau

Elle Daviau

Checkmate

I lost you
and I know it wasn't on purpose
but it hurt.
You didn't even consider me
all you cared about was her.

   That's a lie.

Your feelings for me were a curse.
But when you didn't think about the
consequences
you didn't realize that you had already
lost me first.

Elle Daviau

It's Been Done

Traveling through my anger and rage,
                 bypassing the depths of Hell
to reach forgiveness;
but now I know,
I can never
forgive you.

Elle Daviau

The Boy Gave the Girl a Slice of Watermelon From Their Picnic

My eyes are on fire
and these tears aren't
taking the burn away.

My chest is collapsed
and my short breaths are
taking everything I have for you
and throwing it all away.

Elle Daviau

Senza Nome

Wherever you go,
the moon will always
stay the same.
So when you look up at the stars,
search for my moon, and
it will help you remember my name.

Elle Daviau

Elle Daviau

Magenta Tides.

I think my love is a lot like drowning.
The struggle,
                    giving in,

            and a slow
peaceful end

    when you decide
    to release me into oblivion.

Elle Daviau

Elle Davian

To: My Sweet Apple Pie

Careful which words you make a joke
out of because the ones you throw around
so carelessly,
are often the ones that will push her
to make her decision
of if she will stand up for herself
and walk away
leaving you stuck in the canopy of doubt,
plagued with your bad insecurity.
Or, if she will let you hurt her,
time and time again, with not a word ever
crossing her
luna-tied mouth.

Elle Daviau

Elle Daviau

Fire in My Eyes, Stars in Yours

I may be your hurricane, but you are
still the thorn in my heart that draws
me to the center of
the galaxy.
You hold me in, with all the stars in
your eyes, my tears burn down
my face
when you kiss me
goodnight.

Elle Daviau

Pink Taffy in My Mouth

The lights are burning
my sensitive green eyes,
all because of you.

Elle Daviau

Elle Davian

Try Not to Keep Your Enemies Around.

Because every time I turn around.
You're holding a knife,
ready to drive it
into my back.

Elle Daviau

When I Made You My Religion

I'll just let him
      paint my mind
      and contort my
      memories into the
      static fallout that
      I know, and you think
      you love.
      Then I'll be
        just
       like you.
        The way you like it.

Elle Daviau

Thunder Moon

I can't help but remember
our beautiful memories.
They're a tragic movie
that I just won't stop
rehearsing in my head.

Elle Daviau

The Age of Aquarius.

It's different, the feeling.
Living like I know I'll see you
tomorrow.

Elle Daviau

Opalescent 🌙

true heart break,
true regret,
it takes it all
for him to feel real
again.

Elle Daviau

The Sea Has a Spirit

After it all happened
you reflected you were mine.
My emotions cut through my eyes
and bled the tears I've been saving
for a lifetime.

Not only did I conclude that you would never
shatter the glass
encased beneath my collarbones, but I knew
you could never edge on the side of fault,
the fault that will always be mine.

Elle Daviau

liquid sugar sky

You're attracted to the poison
that kills you,
    drawing you in like sugar
until it touches your tongue,

    draining the blood that ran in my mouth
and when it did, I gave it all to him.

    These are the men that slit your throat with
every kiss. Tearing at your heart
    every single time.

    I didn't realize it then, but I had to go all the
way down with him
    to come back to who I am.

Elle Daviau

Elle Daviau

la fin

This is the beautiful tragedy of how I became to be me.

I noticed something. It's dark, not the way it used to be.

At first it was just one man. He came and went, then another, and another walked into my life.

Their words were poison,
  laced with lies.

Elle Daviau

About the Author

Elle Daviau attends college in the Pacific Northwest. She paints and writes poetry when she is not in a lecture or pondering life's answers in the starlit sky. This is her first poetry book.

Author website: http://www.elledaviau.com

CPSIA information can be obtained
at www.ICGtesting.com
Printed in the USA
BVHW081733291121
622774BV00001B/109

9 781943 337828